I0814017

American Indians

THE CHEROKEE

by N.C. Barnes

DiscoverRoo

An Imprint of Pop!
popbooksonline.com

This book is filled with videos, puzzles, games, and more! Scan the QR codes* while you read, or visit the website below to make this book pop.

popbooksonline.com/Cherokee

abdobooks.com

Published by Pop!, a division of ABDO, PO Box 398166, Minneapolis, Minnesota 55439.

Printed in the United States of America, North Mankato, Minnesota.

052024
082024

Cover Photo: The Canadian Press/Associated Press

Interior Photos: Shutterstock Images, Getty Images, Alamy Stock Photo, Associated Press, Tulsa World/Associated Press, Danita Delimont Photography/Newscom, Don and Melinda Crawford/UCG/Universal Images Group/Newscom

Editor: Emily Dreher

Series Designer: Colleen McLaren

Library of Congress Control Number: 2023947498

Publisher's Cataloging-in-Publication Data

Names: Barnes, N.C., author.

Title: The Cherokee / by N.C. Barnes

Description: Minneapolis, Minnesota : Pop!, 2025 | Series: American Indians | Includes online resources and index

Identifiers: ISBN 9781098246204 (lib. bdg.) | ISBN 9781098246761 (ebook)

Subjects: LCSH: Cherokee Indians--Juvenile literature. | American Indians--Juvenile literature. | Indians of North America--Juvenile literature. | Indigenous peoples--Social life and customs--Juvenile literature. | Cultural anthropology--Juvenile literature.

Classification: DDC 973.0497--dc23

*Scanning QR codes requires a web-enabled smart device with a QR code reader app and a camera.

TABLE OF CONTENTS

CHAPTER 1

WHO ARE THE CHEROKEE?

Before European **settlers** came to North America, the land was wild and open. It was populated by American Indians. Each group had its own languages and **culture**.

The Cherokee people make up a nation. In the nation there are seven **clans** called Wolf, Deer, Bird, Paint, Long Hair, Blue, and Wild Potato.

A Cherokee woman looks over her homeland, the Great Smoky Mountains of North Carolina, in 1942.

CHEROKEE HOMELANDS

HISTORICAL CHEROKEE TERRITORY

The Cherokee lived in specific parts of the highlighted area.

DID YOU KNOW?

The Cherokee people lived in a section of the Appalachian Mountains called the Great Smoky Mountains.

Cherokee people lived in the Appalachian Mountains for thousands of years. They resided in modern day Tennessee, Virginia, West Virginia, Kentucky, North Carolina, South Carolina, Georgia, and Alabama. Their land was covered in mountains and forests.

The Cherokee called their home mountains Shaconage, *meaning "place of blue smoke."*

HISTORICAL LIFE

Cherokee people lived in wattle and daub houses. The walls were made of woven sticks covered in mud or clay. The roofs were **thatched**. The Cherokee made

The woven sticks are the wattle. Daubing is the process of covering the walls with mud or clay.

their beds on benches built into the walls. In the summer, they stayed in large, airy rectangular homes.

LEARN MORE HERE!

Winter houses constantly had fires burning. They got very smoky.

In the winter, Cherokee moved in to dome-shaped houses. These houses were built partly underground. This helped the house stay warm in cold weather. There was a hole in the roof to let out some smoke from the fire.

Cherokee **clans** lived on **fertile** land. Women planted gardens of corn, squash, beans, potatoes, sunflowers, and pumpkins. They also gathered berries, fruits, nuts, and herbs from the wilderness around them.

Cherokee people made jewelry from shells, bones, and wooden beads.

Bows and arrows were made of materials found in nature.

Cherokee teachings focused on a balance with the natural world. They didn't kill too many animals.

Men were the hunters. They used bows and arrows to hunt bears, turkeys, deer, and fish. They also fished with spears, traps, and nets made of plant fibers. For smaller animals such as rabbits and grouse, Cherokee hunted with blowguns and darts. Blowgun tubes were made of river cane.

Cherokee style moccasins have a pucker. The material of the shoe is bunched together at the toe.

Clothes varied depending on the seasons. Since summers were hot and humid, men wore only **breechcloths** and moccasins. Women wore light skirts, and kids were unclothed.

In the winter, men wore animal skin leggings and shirts. Women wore warmer skirts and dresses made from deerskin and mulberry bark. Fur robes were added for extra warmth.

American Indians usually wore their most decorated clothing for important ceremonies.

CHAPTER 3

FAMILY AND TRADITIONS

Cherokee people saw members of their **clans** as family. Individual families lived together in their homes. Specific Cherokee traditions varied from clan to clan. However, all Cherokee people deeply respected their family.

EXPLORE LINKS HERE!

Cherokees believed spirits of family members who were killed couldn't rest until their families **avenged** the crime. The whole village had to agree to go to war. When they did, war parties were made of 20 to 40 men and one woman. The woman watched over captives and cooked for the war party.

The Cherokee wore white feathers in their hair during war.

Children learned from their older family members. Boys learned to hunt and fish from their fathers and uncles. Their uncles decided when a boy could go to war and help make decisions for the family. Girls were taught **homemaking** and gardening skills from their mothers. They also learned how to lead the family.

CHEROKEE LANGUAGE

Sequoyah was the son of a Cherokee mother and European father. He worked to make a writing system for the Cherokee language. It took him 12 years. He created 86 symbols to represent the sounds of the Cherokee language. Sequoyah's symbols helped many Cherokee learn to read and write. The writing system is still in use today.

After contact with Europeans, Cherokee people started wearing some cotton clothes.

Both Cherokee men and women crafted things. Men made weapons, nets, and dugout canoes. These canoes were built from tulip poplar trees. The trees needed to have a large, straight trunk.

Dugout canoes are carved using a burn-and-scrape technique.

The trunks were hollowed out with fire and carved into a canoe shape. The long process took much skill. Women wove baskets from river cane and white oak.

CHAPTER 4

TRAIL OF TEARS TO TODAY

In 1540, the Cherokee first saw Europeans. The nation controlled most of the land in the southern parts of the Appalachian Mountains at the time. Soon, the Europeans pressured Cherokee **clans** to give up their land. It was the start of massive **displacement** of the Cherokee.

COMPLETE AN ACTIVITY HERE!

There are many pieces of art that show the Cherokee during their displacement in the 1800s.

In 1830, US Congress passed the Indian Removal Act. It let President Andrew Jackson trade **unsettled** land west of the Mississippi River for the Cherokee people's land. Many Cherokee refused to leave. Their nation had lived there for thousands of years. Eventually, the US government forcibly removed them.

Dirt in the Cherokee's new home in Oklahoma is red. It has a lot of iron in it.

Museums have artifacts that document the displacement of American Indians.

DID YOU KNOW?

Settlers found gold in Cherokee territory. That was a reason that they forced Cherokees from their homeland.

To honor the Cherokee, US Congress made the Trail of Tears a National Historic Trail in 1987.

After being forced off their traditional homelands, Cherokee people were offered unsettled land in the west. They were forced to walk 800 miles (1,287km) from the Appalachian Mountains to Oklahoma. This walk is called the Trail of Tears. About 4,000 Cherokee Nation members died during the journey.

Cherokee **culture** has survived despite the challenges. Today, they are one of the largest nations in the United States. There are three officially recognized Cherokee tribes. They are in North Carolina and Oklahoma. These tribes are the Eastern Band of Cherokee Indians, the Cherokee Nation, and the United Keetoowah Band of Cherokee Indians.

Wilma Mankiller was the first woman to be elected as Principal Chief of the Cherokee Nation.

MAKING CONNECTIONS

TEXT-TO-SELF

Cherokee children learned skills from their parents and family members. Have you learned any skills that way?

TEXT-TO-TEXT

Have you read about another American Indian nation? How is their culture similar to or different from the Cherokee people?

TEXT-TO-WORLD

Cherokee people were forced from their homeland after the Indian Removal Act. Can you think of any other groups of people who were forced from their homes? How was their experience similar to or different from the Cherokee?

GLOSSARY

avenge — to punish a person or group for wrongdoing.

breechcloth — a cloth worn over the groin.

ceremony — a formal event held on a special occasion.

clan — a group of people tracing descent from a common ancestor.

culture — the customs, arts, and ideas of a group of people.

displacement — the act of forcing people to flee from their home or homeland.

fertile — producing plentiful crops.

homemaking — caring for a household by cooking, cleaning, and raising children.

settler — a person who moves with a group of others to live in a new country or area. A place where settlers live is called a settlement.

thatched — made from layering plant material.

unsettled — not lived in by settlers.

INDEX

DiscoverRoo!
ONLINE RESOURCES

This book is filled with videos, puzzles, games, and more! Scan the QR codes* while you read, or visit the website below to make this book pop.

popbooksonline.com/Cherokee

*Scanning QR codes requires a web-enabled smart device with a QR code reader app and a camera.